Why do mammals have fur?

And other questions about evolution and classification

W
FRANKLIN WATTS
LONDON • SYDNEY

Franklin Watts

This edition copyright © Franklin Watts 2016

IBSN 978 14451 5088 8

Dewey: 599

A CIP catalogue record for this book is
available from the British Library.

Series Editor: Julia Bird

Packaged by: Dynamo Limited

Picture credits

Key: **t**=top, **m**=middle, **b**=bottom, **l**=left, **r**=right

Cover: Eric Isselee/Shutterstock, Kontur-vid/Shutterstock; p1 Eric Isselee/Shutterstock; p3 Kontur-vid/Shutterstock;
p4 **t** Linda Bucklin/Shutterstock; p4 **b** Erni/Shutterstock; p5 **t** Eric Isselee/Shutterstock; p5 **b** Sfocato/Shutterstock;
p7 (rabbit) Leena Robinson/Shutterstock; p8 **t** Eric Gevaert/Shutterstock; p8 **b** MartinMaritz/Shutterstock; p9 **t** Dan Cox;
p9 **b** Susan Flashman/Shutterstock; p10 **t** Steve Downer/Ardea; p10 **b** Yulia Avgust/Shutterstock; p11 **t** Vaclav Volrab/
Shutterstock; p11 **b** Christian Musat/Shutterstock; p12 Shchipkova Elena/Shutterstock; p13 **t** Vladimir Wrangel/Shutterstock;
p13 **b** Sergey Krasnoshchokov/Shutterstock; p14 **t** Paul Mozell/Shutterstock; p14 **b** Jason Kasumovic/Shutterstock;
p15 **t** John Braid/Shutterstock; p15 **b** Dan Cox; p16 **t** Peter Krejzl/Shutterstock; p16 **b** Pannochka/Shutterstock;
p17 **t** Hedrus/Shutterstock; p17 **bl** BMJ/Shutterstock; **br** AdStock RF/Shutterstock; p18 **tl** DDCoral/Shutterstock;
p18 **tr** Dynamo; p18 **b** cheetah Eric Isselee/Shutterstock; p19 **tl** Andrew Lam/Shutterstock; p19 **tr** Hammett79/Shutterstock;
p19 **b** Hung Chung Chih/Shutterstock; p20 **t** Nacho Such/Shutterstock; p20 **b** Liquid Productions, LLC/Shutterstock;
p21 **t** Kirsanov Valeriy Vladimirovich/Shutterstock; p21 **m** Jean Michel Labat/Ardea; p21 **b** Christopher Meder/Shutterstock;
p22 **t** MarclSchauer/Shutterstock; p22 **b** Niall Dunne/Shutterstock; p23 Four Oaks/Shutterstock; p24 **t** Wildnerdpix/Shutterstock;
p24 **b** Photodynamic/Shutterstock; p25 **t** Daleen Loest/Shutterstock; p25 **b** AndreAnita/Shutterstock; p26 Mariusz Potocki/
Shutterstock; p27 **t** Eric Isselee/Shutterstock; p27 **b** Eduard Kyslynskyy/Shutterstock; p28 **b** John Carnemolla/Shutterstock;
p29 **t** Eric Gevaert/Shutterstock; p29 **b** Keith + Liz Laidler/Ardea; p30 **t** Szente A/Shutterstock; p30 **b** Nobusuke Oki/Shutterstock

Printed in China

Franklin Watts
An imprint of
Hachette Children's Group
Part of The Watts Publishing Group
Carmelite House
50 Victoria Embankment
London EC4Y 0DZ

An Hachette UK Company
www.hachette.co.uk

www.franklinwatts.co.uk

FSC
www.fsc.org
MIX
Paper from
responsible sources
FSC® C104740

Every effort has been made by the Publishers to ensure that the websites in this book are suitable for children, and that they contain no inappropriate or offensive
material. However, because of the nature of the Internet, it is impossible to guarantee that the contents of these sites will not be altered. We strongly advise that
Internet access is supervised by a responsible adult.

Contents

What is a mammal?

Mammals are warm-blooded animals. This means that they can keep their bodies at the same temperature by burning food to keep warm. Mammals breathe air and most have hair on their bodies. Mammal mothers all produce milk to feed their babies.

This mammal-like reptile, named Estemmenosuchus, lived 255 million years ago.

How mammals evolved

Mammals are descended from mammal-like **reptiles** that lived around 260 million years ago. Most of these creatures had died out by the start of the Mesozoic era (the age of the dinosaurs) but a few survived and developed into the first true mammals.

The first true mammals were similar to modern-day shrews.

The first mammals

The first real mammals were shrew-like animals that lived alongside the dinosaurs and probably ate insects. Because they were warm-blooded, they were able to hunt at night, when the **cold-blooded** dinosaurs were asleep. The little mammals developed good senses of smell and hearing so they could find their prey in the dark.

TIMELINE: CENOZOIC ERA

MESOZOIC ERA: 252–66 million years ago (mya)	Paleocene 65–56 mya			Eocene 56–34 mya	
		60	**50**		**40**

Mammals inherit the Earth

At the end of the Mesozoic era, a catastrophic event wiped out all the dinosaurs. Most scientists believe that an **asteroid** struck the Earth and sent up a huge cloud of dust, which blocked out the Sun so plants could not grow. Without competition from the dinosaurs, the little mammals quickly **evolved** into many different groups.

Mammals are the only animals that suckle their babies.

Smilodon is one of the best-known sabre-toothed cats. It lived during the Pleistocene epoch.

THE AGE OF MAMMALS

Oligocene 34–23 mya

Miocene 23–5 mya

Pliocene 5–1.8 mya

Pleistocene 1.8 mya–10,000 ya

Holocene 10,000 ya–now

30

20

10

Classification of mammals

There are more than 5,000 **species** of living mammals. They are divided into about 21 groups. As well as those shown below, there are other groups made up of just one or two species. These are the colugos (flying lemurs), aardvarks, hyraxes and elephant shrews.

Even-toed hoofed animals

These mammals carry their weight on their third and fourth toes. They include deer, pigs, cows, sheep, hippos and giraffes.

Odd-toed hoofed animals

This group includes horses, zebras, rhinos and tapirs. They carry most of their weight on their third toe.

Carnivores

The meat-eating mammals differ in size more than any other group. They include weasels, cats, dogs and bears.

Whales, dolphins and porpoises

These mammals, called cetaceans, have adapted to a life spent entirely in water, making them one of the most highly specialised groups.

Bats

Bats are divided into megabats, which eat fruit and nectar and do not have **echolocation**, and microbats that use echolocation and feed on insects.

Insect-eaters

Insectivores survive mainly on **protein**-rich insects and worms. This group includes hedgehogs, moles and shrews.

Rodents

More than 40 per cent of mammals are rodents. Their teeth never stop growing so they need to gnaw constantly to keep them short.

Rabbits, hares, pikas

These mammals are similar to rodents. Their teeth grow all through their lives but, unlike rodents, they have two extra 'peg teeth' behind their top **incisors**.

Pangolins

Pangolins are the only mammals that have scales instead of fur. They use their long claws to dig up anthills and termite nests for food.

Primates

Primates have eyes that face forwards and most have five fingers and toes with **opposable thumbs**. They include monkeys, apes, lemurs and humans.

Elephants

African and Indian elephants are the only surviving species from a group of mammals with trunks that included the woolly mammoth.

Sea cows

Dugongs and manatees make up this group of **aquatic** mammals that graze on sea grass and other underwater plants.

Fin-footed mammals

Seals, sea lions and walruses are semi-aquatic – adapted to living on land during the breeding season and spending months at sea.

Sloths, anteaters and armadillos

Only found in the Americas, these mammals had huge **prehistoric** relatives – the giant ground sloths and the tank-like **glyptodonts**.

Marsupials

Marsupials give birth to undeveloped babies that grow in their mothers' pouches, instead of inside their bodies. They include kangaroos, koalas and opossums.

Monotremes

The duck-billed platypus and the echidna are monotremes. They are the only mammals that lay eggs, but they still feed their babies on milk.

Birth and growth

Most mammal babies develop inside their mother's body before they are born. Some mammal mothers have single babies, while others give birth to large **litters**. Mammals care for their young until they are ready to look after themselves.

Orangutans stay with their mothers until they are ten years old. They have lots to learn before they can live alone.

With so many predators about, wildebeest babies need to be ready to run soon after birth.

Growing up

Some mammal babies, including zebras and wildebeest, are on their feet within minutes of being born. Others, such as rats, are born blind and hairless, so their mother builds a nest to protect them. Mice leave their nests after a few weeks and are ready to breed at six weeks old. More intelligent animals have to learn a lot of skills before they can look after themselves, so they stay with their mothers for years. In general, larger animals live longer than small creatures. Bowhead whales may live for more than 200 years.

Egg-laying mammals

An unusual group of mammals called monotremes (see page 7) lay eggs, but feed their babies on milk after they hatch. The only surviving species are the duck-billed platypus, which lives in Australia, and the echidna, found in Australia and New Guinea.

Platypus eggs take ten days to hatch. The babies are the size of a butter bean and quite helpless.

Marsupial babies

A group of mammals called marsupials give birth to tiny, blind and furless babies that climb into their mother's pouch, where they attach themselves to a nipple and drink milk. The babies, called joeys, stay in the pouch for weeks or months depending on the species. Almost all marsupials live in Australia and South America.

A baby koala lives in its mother's pouch for about six months.

9

All shapes and sizes

Most of the earliest mammals were the size of mice, but during the Eocene epoch (56–34 mya), the climate grew warmer, grasslands appeared and mammals became supersized. They included Paraceratherium, the biggest land mammal that ever lived. Most mega-mammals died out thousands of years ago. Today more than 95 per cent of mammals are smaller than we are.

The tiny bumblebee bat measures just 30 mm from nose to tail.

Smallest mammal

There are two contenders for the title of tiniest mammal: the bumblebee bat, which lives in caves in Thailand and Burma, and the Etruscan shrew, which weighs just 1.8 grams. Small mammals burn food fast, so they need a **nutritious** diet. Both these creatures eat insects, which are high in protein.

Biggest mammal

The blue whale is the largest creature ever to have lived. This record-breaking mammal feeds on tiny fish and shellfish, and can swallow up to four tonnes a day. Such a heavy creature could never survive on land. It is only able to grow so large because the water supports its weight.

Largest living land mammal

The elephant is the largest land mammal alive today, but it would have been dwarfed by its prehistoric **ancestor** Elephas recki, which stood a metre higher at the shoulder.

Elephants have legs like pillars and cushioned pads on the soles of their feet to support their weight.

Tallest living mammal

A giraffe's towering height allows it to feed on leaves that are out of reach of other animals, and helps it to spot predators. Male giraffes wrestle using their necks and the strongest usually gets his pick of the females. It is possible that in prehistoric times, when giraffes had shorter necks, those with the longest necks won these battles to breed. In this case, the winner's babies would also have longer necks.

A blue whale's tongue can weigh as much as an elephant and its heart is the size of a car.

Giraffes have seven neck vertebrae (bones), just like we do, but each one is 25.5 cm long.

Adapting to extremes

Mammals have adapted their bodies and behaviour to live in almost all parts of the world, from scorched deserts to icy seas. The only places mammals cannot survive are the deepest oceans, the highest mountain peaks, the driest deserts and the frozen wastes of inland Antarctica.

Coping with the cold

Mammals that live in freezing climates have a deep layer of fat or blubber and usually have thick fur to protect them from the cold. Some, such as the Arctic fox, even have furry feet that allow them to walk on the ice. Another way that mammals survive harsh winters is by **hibernating** underground during the coldest months.

Polar bears have two layers of fur and a thick layer of fat to keep them warm. Their small ears and tail reduce heat loss.

Surviving the heat

Mammals that live in hot environments often hide away in underground dens during the day and come out to feed at dusk or dawn. Others are **nocturnal** and have developed special features to help them find food in the dark, such as huge eyes or echolocation. Some mammals, including elephants, have large ears that help them to get rid of excess body heat.

Fennec foxes spend the day in dens beneath the desert sand. Their huge ears give off heat and help to keep them cool.

Long distance travellers

Caribou, also called reindeer, escape the worst of the Arctic winter by migrating hundreds of kilometres to more sheltered regions. Their hooves are adapted to life in the deep freeze – they have sharp edges to stop them slipping on ice, and are hollowed out like a scoop to help them dig through the snow to find food.

As the first snows fall, large herds of caribou head south from their summer feeding grounds in the Arctic tundra.

Changing the landscape

While most animals adapt to their habitats, there are some that change the environment to suit their needs.

Beavers are rodents and use their powerful front teeth to gnaw through tree trunks. They can fell several trees in a single night.

Busy beavers

Beavers live in lodges made of mud and branches in the middle of ponds – and if a pond is not available, beavers create their own by building a dam to block a river. Working at night, beavers fell trees and use the wood to make their dams and lodges. They eat tree bark, roots, leaves and water plants, so the tree stumps are also a useful source of food when they grow new shoots.

Beavers are excellent swimmers thanks to their webbed hind feet and paddle-shaped tails.

Human eco engineers

Archaeologists have uncovered the remains of human camps dating back 750,000 years. By building shelters, wearing the hides of other mammals and discovering fire, early humans were able to move to cooler parts of the world. Since then, we have become the ultimate engineers, changing the environment so much that the survival of other species is put at risk.

Skara Brae is a stone-built, Neolithic village on the west coast of Scotland. People lived here between 3200BCE and 2200BCE.

Prairie dog cities

Prairie dogs live in vast underground burrows called towns, with lots of entrances, marked by mounds of packed earth. These towns contain nurseries, sleeping quarters, toilets and listening posts close to the entrances, all linked by tunnels. The largest known town, in Texas, USA, extended to 65,000 sq km and housed up to 400 million prairie dogs.

Guards keep watch from the mounds outside prairie dog towns, ready to give a warning cry if predators are nearby.

Hair and skin

Fossil footprints made 250 million years ago suggest that the mammals' direct ancestors had a covering of hair. Fur protects a mammal's skin from the Sun, from injury and from extreme cold.

Mammals that live in cold climates, such as the musk-ox, have an undercoat of thick fur beneath an outer layer of guard hairs.

Hairless mammals

Almost all mammals – including humans – have hairy skin, but some aquatic mammals have a thick layer of blubber instead of a furry coat to keep them warm. Hippos and armadillos are almost hairless, while pangolins have scales in place of fur.

Dolphins are often born with a few hairs sticking out of their chin, but these soon fall out.

Each zebra's stripes are different, which may help them to recognise one another.

Clever camouflage

Some animals have patterned coats that make it hard for predators – or prey – to spot them. A zebra's black and white stripes may stand out to us, but lions do not see colours as we do and are confused by the pattern, which makes it difficult to pick out an individual animal in a herd.

Changing colour

Mammals from colder regions sometimes change colour in winter, so that they are less easy to spot in the snow. The Arctic fox and Arctic hare both exchange their brown coats for white as winter approaches.

In winter, the Arctic fox grows a thick, white coat, so it blends into the snowy landscape.

Different diets

Mammals need to eat a lot. Some plant eaters, including cows, have four stomachs so they can get maximum nutrition from their food. Others, such as elephants, have less efficient digestive systems. Seeds and plant material pass through their bodies untouched and provide important food for birds and dungbeetles.

Mammals with four stomachs, such as this cow, are called ruminants.

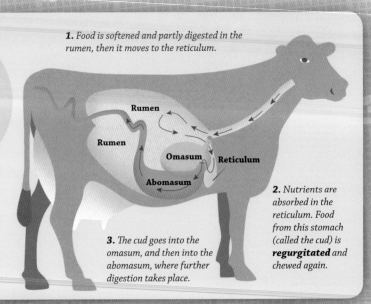

1. *Food is softened and partly digested in the rumen, then it moves to the reticulum.*

Rumen

Rumen

Omasum   Reticulum

Abomasum

2. *Nutrients are absorbed in the reticulum. Food from this stomach (called the cud) is **regurgitated** and chewed again.*

3. *The cud goes into the omasum, and then into the abomasum, where further digestion takes place.*

Food chains

Food chains begin with a plant and end with a predator. In a simple food chain, grass is eaten by a zebra, which is then eaten by a lion. It is thought that the dinosaurs died out because the plants stopped growing. The plant-eating dinosaurs died of starvation and when the meat-eaters had eaten all bodies of the plant-eaters, they died too.

Cheetahs are carnivores and only eat meat. This one has caught an impala, which is a plant eater.

Teeth are the clue

Scientists work out what an animal ate by looking at its teeth. Most **herbivores** have large, flat teeth that grind down tough plants. Carnivores have long **canines** for holding onto prey and sharp, narrow teeth for slicing and tearing flesh. **Omnivores** eat meat and plants so their teeth are a mixture of the two.

A carnivore's teeth are sharp and pointed (left), while a herbivore's teeth are flat (right). To see an omnivore's teeth, take a look in your own mouth.

Pandas must eat up to 38 kg of bamboo each day to meet their energy needs.

Picky eaters

Although giant pandas are classed as carnivores, their diet is made up almost entirely of bamboo. Koalas – which are marsupials, not bears – live on eucalyptus and have developed an especially long digestive system to break down the tough leaves. Both these mammals are endangered by their restricted diets as the Chinese bamboo forests and the Australian woodlands continue to shrink.

Mammals on the move

Since Mesozoic mammals scurried at the feet of the dinosaurs, mammals have developed a number of different ways of getting about. The fastest mammal is the cheetah, which can accelerate from 0 to 100 kph in just three seconds. The slowest mover is the sloth, with a top speed of under 2 kph.

The sloth moves so little that its fur gets covered by tiny plants called algae, which make it look slightly green.

Manatees are slow swimmers. They eat underwater plants and have no natural predators so they do not need to move quickly.

Taking to the water

Aquatic mammals, such as whales, dolphins and manatees, are descended from animals that lived on land and once had four limbs. Their forelegs became flippers and their hind limbs disappeared. These mammals still have lungs and need to surface to breathe.

Fliers and gliders

The oldest known bat lived during the early Eocene epoch. It could fly but had not developed echolocation, so it relied on other senses to find its way and locate prey. Bats are the only mammals that can truly fly. Creatures such as the flying squirrel use a flap of skin between their front and hind legs to glide between trees.

Bats are aerial acrobats. They have thin, flexible wings, so they can change direction more quickly than birds.

Spider monkeys spend most of their time in the trees and use their long arms and tails to swing through the forest.

Treetop swingers

Some apes and monkeys move swiftly through the trees by using their arms to swing from branch to branch. Certain mammals, including spider monkeys, have developed **prehensile** tails that can grasp or hold onto objects like an extra arm and hand.

Leaps and bounds

Kangaroos are the most energy-efficient travellers over long distances. Red kangaroos can hop at speeds of up to 60 kph and leap an incredible seven metres, powered by strong, elastic **tendons** in their legs. They use their tail as a counterbalance – its downward thrust helps to propel the kangaroo back into the air.

Kangaroos cannot move one leg without the other, so they have no choice but to hop.

Animal intelligence

Humans' brains began to grow larger about five million years ago and we like to believe that we are the smartest creatures on Earth. However, recent studies suggest that other mammals are just as clever, but in different ways – and some can even outsmart us.

Chimps and humans probably evolved from the same ancestor about eight million years ago.

Champion chimp

In a test at Kyoto University in 2007, a young male chimpanzee was able to remember a series of nine numbers and tap them in on a touch screen in the right order, even though the numbers had been shown for just a fraction of a second. He outperformed a group of university students and even beat the British memory champion.

Supersmart cetaceans

When it comes to intelligence, dolphins are second only to humans. They have reasoning ability, understand sign language, mimic (copy) behaviour and communicate using clicks and whistles. In addition, they have developed the skill of echolocation. By emitting a series of clicks that bounce back from solid objects, dolphins use sound waves to build up a picture of their underwater environment.

Dolphins have larger brains than humans and learn very quickly.

Brainy beasts

An elephant's brain is larger than that of any other land mammal. Like chimps and dolphins, elephants use tools – they will find a stick to scratch an itch and have been known to drop rocks onto electric fences to break them. Elephants live in tightly-knit family groups and will grieve for days when a member dies. They are famous for having long memories and still show signs of mourning years later if they pass the spot where the death occurred.

Elephants have a sense of humour and like to play. Squirting water from their trunks is a favourite game.

Social behaviour

While many mammals live in groups, some rarely spend time with one other except when mating or raising young. These animals are usually **territorial** and will fight off any intruders. Living alone means they do not have to share food or space with others.

Some big animals, such as bears, need a lot of food to survive, so they prefer not to share their territories with others.

Colony dwellers

Mammals that live in colonies usually help one another out. One member will keep watch while others feed and an adult will act as a babysitter for the young. If there are group members that cannot hunt, others will often share their food.

Meerkats live in colonies of up to 50 animals. The group is ruled by the strongest female and her chosen mate.

Team players

Pack hunters, such as wolves, have evolved to join forces to catch their prey. By working together as a team, they can bring down animals far larger than themselves. Some packs develop clever hunting tactics where each member has a role to play. Others overwhelm their prey by sheer weight of numbers.

African hunting dogs are among the most successful pack hunters. Almost 80 per cent of their hunts end in a kill, compared to 30 per cent in the case of lions.

Wildebeest gather in herds of up to 1.5 million as they cross the Mara river in search of fresh grazing.

Huge herds

Grazing mammals often form huge herds as protection from predators. When many animals are gathered together, the risk to each individual is less than if it were alone. Young animals can be protected in the centre of the group and there are many pairs of eyes to watch for danger. Wildebeest, for example, often take turns sleeping while other herd members stand guard.

Exchanging information

Spoken language first developed among humans between 100,000 and 30,000 years ago. This sets us apart from the rest of the animal kingdom, but other mammals still communicate, using sound, scent and body language.

Sound

Many mammals use sound as a mating call, warning or to communicate with their young. Prairie dogs have developed various warning barks that give information about the type of predator, its colour, direction and speed. Howler monkeys' calls can be heard over five kilometres away as groups stake their claim to a patch of rainforest.

Seals gather in large colonies to give birth, so it is important that mothers and pups recognise each other's calls. Otherwise, a mother might feed the wrong baby.

Scent

Scent is one of the most basic ways that animals communicate with one another and many have a far better sense of smell that we do. Mammals often have **glands** that leave their scent in places they have visited, to mark their territory and warn off intruders. Scent can also be used to signal that they are ready to mate.

This snarling leopard is displaying its impressive teeth as a warning that it can inflict a powerful bite.

Body language

Mammals often use body language as a warning or to show who is boss. An **alpha** male carries his head high, with his ears erect. A weaker male lowers his head, puts his ears back and tucks his tail between his legs. Many mammals bare their teeth when they are angry to warn others to back off. If elephants are about to charge they pull their ears forward, stare intensely and stamp their feet.

Continuing evolution

Animals are constantly adapting to new challenges, including **climate change**, loss of habitat and human activities. For example, some elephants are born without tusks and the number is increasing. This could be because ivory poachers kill elephants for their tusks and those that do not have tusks survive to breed.

Extinction

When mammals are no longer able to survive changing conditions, the species becomes extinct. Most creatures die out after a few million years, but a few have survived almost unchanged since prehistoric times. This is because they are perfectly adapted to their environment and have few competitors for food and space. They are called 'living fossils' and include the elephant shrew and the echidna (below).

Echidnas are egg-laying mammals, like the platypus. Scientists believe that they both evolved from the same ancestor about 30 million years ago.

Conservation

Many countries have national parks where animals are protected from human threats such as hunting, mining and farming. Where species are on the brink of extinction, zoos run breeding programmes in the hope that endangered animals can be reintroduced to the wild. This has been successful in the case of the bison, the golden lion tamarin (right) and Przewalski's horse among others.

In 1969, just 150 golden lion tamarins were known to exist in the wild. Now, thanks to conservation programmes, there are more than 1,600.

Endangered mammals

At least one in four mammals is at risk of extinction in the near future. The Amur leopard is among the world's rarest animals. It is threatened by illegal hunting, forest fires and climate change. The Sumatran rhinoceros is also critically endangered. It is hunted for its horn and its forest habitat is being destroyed to make way for palm oil plantations.

The pangolin is endangered because its meat is a delicacy in China and its scales are used in traditional medicine.

Amazing mammals

Mammals are fascinating, whatever their size, shape or lifestyle. Here are just a few of the many fantastic facts about these awesome animals.

Giant beaver dam

The world's biggest beaver dam, in Alberta, Canada, measured 850 metres across and could be seen from space.

Big teeth

Elephants' back teeth are the size of a brick and weigh two kilograms. They are replaced six times during the animal's lifetime.

Noisiest mammal

The blue whale is the noisiest animal on Earth. Its calls are louder than a jet engine and can carry for 800 km.

Massive tongue

Giraffes have prehensile, purple-black tongues that are 50 centimetres long. They are perfect for stripping leaves from trees – and also make handy ear cleaners.

Long sleep

The Arctic ground squirrel (below) spends seven months in hibernation. During this time, its body temperature can fall to minus 3°C.

Longest mammal migration

Each year, grey whales make a round trip of 15,000–20,000 kilometres between their northern feeding grounds and the waters off the coast of Mexico, where they breed.

Black polar bears

Polar bears are not really white. They have black skin covered by colourless, hollow hairs that look white to us because they reflect light in the same way that snow and ice do.

Glossary

Alpha The strongest member of a group

Ancestor An early type of animal from which others have evolved

Aquatic Living in or near water

Archaeologist A scientist who studies prehistoric people by looking at the things they have left behind

Asteroid A small rocky planet

Canines Sharp, pointed teeth used for holding onto food and killing prey

Climate change A change in the weather, often thought to be caused by human activity

Cold-blooded An animal whose body temperature changes according to the surrounding air or water temperature

Echolocation Locating objects by measuring the time it takes for soundwaves to bounce back from them

Evolve To develop gradually over generations

Fossil The preserved remains or impression of animals and plants that died long ago

Gland An organ in the body that produces chemicals, which are used in the body or released into the surroundings

Glyptodont A relative of the armadillo that was the size of a car and lived between 4 million and 10,000 years ago

Herbivores Plant eaters

Hibernating Going into a deep sleep to survive the cold weather when food is scarce

Incisors Front teeth used to cut and tear

Litter A group of babies born to a single mammal at the same time

Nocturnal Active during the night

Nutritious A food that is full of goodness

Omnivore Creature that eats plants and animals

Opposable thumbs Thumbs that can be placed opposite the fingers of the same hand so that it can grasp and handle objects. Primates, including apes and humans, have opposable thumbs.

Predator An animal that hunts other creatures for food

Prehensile A limb, tail or tongue that is able to grasp things

Prehistoric The time before written records

Protein Protein in food builds, repairs and replaces the body's tissues. Meat, fish, eggs and milk are all rich in protein.

Regurgitate Bring food that has already been swallowed back up into the mouth

Reptiles Cold-blooded animals with scaly skin. They include snakes and lizards.

Species A group of animals that can breed with one another and produce healthy babies, which are able to breed when they grow up

Tendons Tough, stretchy bands that connect muscles to bones

Territorial An animal that defends its territory against intruders

Index

Find out more

Here are some useful websites to help you learn more about mammals and evolution.

- 🐾 www.arkive.org
- 🐾 www.wellcometreeoflife.org/interactive
- 🐾 science.discovery.com/games-and-interactives/charles-darwin-game.htm
- 🐾 www.nhm.ac.uk/kids-only
- 🐾 www.oum.ox.ac.uk/thezone/animals